D0844502

We Visit

SAUDI ARABIA

Kathleen
Tracy

Mitchell Lane
PUBLISHERS
P.O. Box 196
Hockessin, Delaware 19707

Afghanistan
Iran
Iraq
Israel
Kuwait
Oman
Pakistan
Saudi Arabia
Turkey
Yemen

Omdurman
Khartoum
Wad Madani
ERITREA
Massawa
Asmara

YOUR LAND AND MY LAND
The Middle East

We Visit

SAUDI ARABIA

Printing 1 2 3 4 5 6 7 8 9

Middle East

Library of Congress Cataloging-in-Publication Data
Tracy, Kathleen.
We visit Saudi Arabia / by Kathleen Tracy.
p. cm. — (Your land and my land—the Middle East)
Includes bibliographical references and index.
ISBN 978-1-58415-963-6 (library bound)
1. Saudi Arabia—Juvenile literature. I. Title.
DS204.25.T73 2011
953.8—dc22

2011000728

eBook ISBN: 9781612280851

PUBLISHER'S NOTE: This story is based on the author's extensive research, which she believes to be accurate. Documentation of this research is on page 60.

To reflect current usage, we have chosen to use the secular era designations BCE ("before the common era") and CE ("of the common era") instead of the traditional designations BC ("before Christ") and AD (anno Domini, "in the year of the Lord").

The Internet sites referenced herein were active as of the publication date. Due to the fleeting nature of some web sites, we cannot guarantee they will all be active when you are reading this book.

PLB

Contents

Introduction ... 6
1 Country Overview ... 9
Where in the World Is Saudi Arabia? ... 12
Saudi Arabia Facts at a Glance ... 13
2 A Brief History ... 15
3 Politics and Government ... 19
4 The Land ... 25
5 The People of Saudi Arabia ... 29
6 Culture and Lifestyle ... 33
7 Saudi Economy and Commerce ... 39
8 Famous Saudi Arabians ... 43
9 Saudi Festivals ... 49
10 Places to Visit in Saudi Arabia ... 53
Saudi Recipes: Saudi Date Sweet and Jiffy Punch ... 56
Saudi Craft: The Feast of Eid al-Fitr ... 57
Timeline ... 58
Chapter Notes ... 59
Further Reading ... 60
Books ... 60
Works Consulted ... 60
On the Internet ... 61
Glossary ... 62
Index ... 63

Introduction

It is the location of the most ancient lands and home to the three most followed religions on earth. It is the birthplace of human civilization and a region torn by nearly continual tribal warfare. It is the inspiration for magical legends and the site of archaeological treasures. It is a devout realm of mosques supported by fields of oil wells. Complex, enigmatic, and compelling, the Middle East is one of the most intriguing and misunderstood areas in the world.

The term *Middle East* is relatively new. For centuries, Europeans referred to the region as the Near East—to distinguish it from the Far East (which includes China, Japan, and other Asian countries). The earliest reference to the Middle East occurred in a 1902 article published in the British journal *National Review*, which noted its location as midway between Great Britain and India.[1]

Afterward, *London Times* journalist Valentine Chirol, who was based in Tehran, popularized the term.[2] The residents initially resisted the term but now accept it as a modern geographical point of reference.

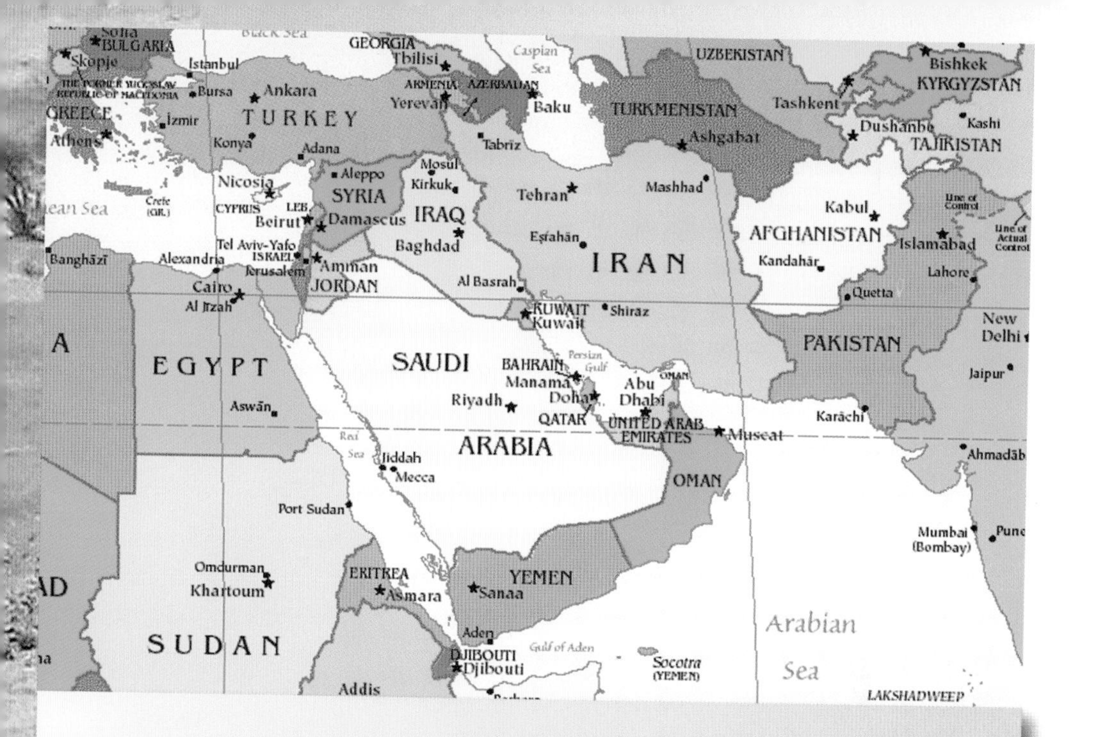

In terms of area, Saudi Arabia is the largest country in the Middle East. Mecca, located in the eastern part of the country, is the spiritual center of the Islamic world.

Even so, there is ongoing debate over which countries comprise the Middle East. The more conservative consensus is that the Middle East is the area bordered by Egypt to the west, the Arabian Sea to the south, and Iran to the east. Some people also include Armenia, Afghanistan, Azerbaijan, and Pakistan because they are predominantly Islamic countries. This series takes the less conservative approach.

Although the Middle Eastern countries share a common language and, most important, a common dominant religion, there are significant differences between the countries, with each having a distinct culture and unique history. In this book we'll explore Saudi Arabia, one of the most religiously and socially conservative countries in the world.

FYI FACT:

Saudi Arabia is named after its ruling family, the Al Sauds.

A satellite photo of the Arabian Peninsula shows the vast stretches of desert in Saudi Arabia.

Chapter 1

Country Overview

Imagine an ocean of pure sand glistening in various shades of gold under the sun for as far as the eye can see, with dunes taller than thirty-story buildings or a land so dry that no rivers can exist. Out of such a seemingly harsh, desolate world, the nomadic Semitic people who lived there would ultimately settle the peninsula and then emigrate to Mesopotamia and Africa. They would be responsible for some of the first great human civilizations, establish three major world religions, and continue to influence both Eastern and Western culture four thousand years later.

Saudi Arabia dominates the Arabian Peninsula, which is part of the Asian continent. The southern portion of the peninsula along the Arabian Sea (which is actually part of the Indian Ocean) spans the countries of Yemen and Oman. This area receives regular rainfall and supports exotic tropical plants and wildlife. It is also the location of the only serviceable commercial port, in Aden, Yemen.

Saudi Arabia, by contrast, is one of the driest places on earth, with a vast sand desert to the east and to the west, arid

mountains, and steppes, which are grassy plains with no trees. While the southern Arabians built cities and relied on agriculture, many northern Arabians—notably the Bedouins—were nomadic and tribal, living an isolated existence. Although Saudi Arabia has several urban areas, the majority of the country remains uninhabited.

The country is divided into thirteen provinces, or emirates. Each has a capital city and is administered by an emir with the rank of minister, who is a member of the ruling royal family. Saudi Arabia is roughly the size of Western Europe—or about a third the size of the United States—with a population similar to the state of Texas. It is a young country with nearly 40 percent of the population under 14 and an overall median age of 25 years old.[1]

In addition to being the homeland of Arab people, Saudi Arabia is the birthplace of Muhammad, who founded Islam, the world's second-largest religion behind Christianity. The Saudi cities of Mecca and Medina are two of the faith's holiest pilgrimage destinations.

You might be surprised to find out that Saudi Arabia uses a lunar calendar that equals 354 days a year instead of 365 days a year. This means that the seasons are not linked to a specific month the way they are in the Gregorian calendar, which is used by Western and non-Muslim nations. In most Muslim countries

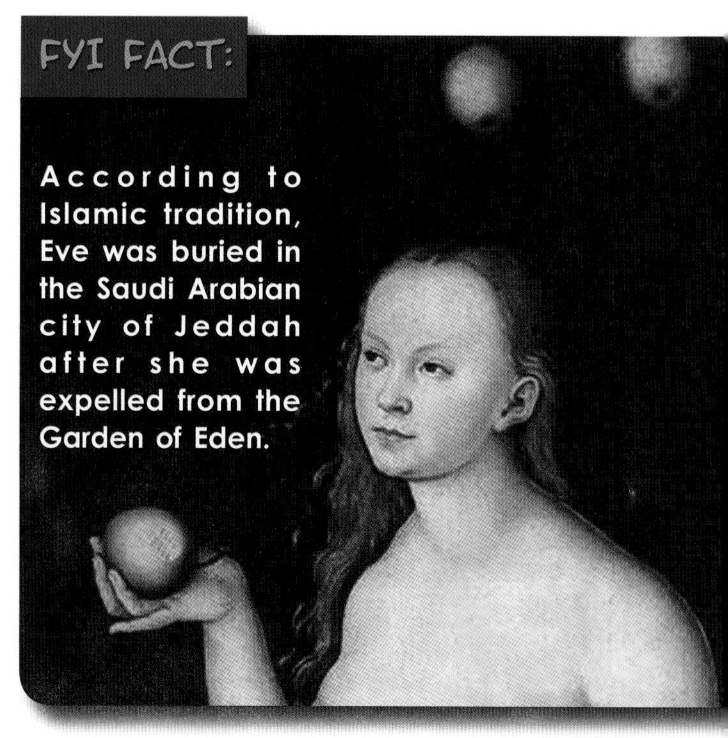

FYI FACT:

According to Islamic tradition, Eve was buried in the Saudi Arabian city of Jeddah after she was expelled from the Garden of Eden.

the Islamic lunar calendar, called the Hijri calendar, is used to determine Islamic holy days and festivals. Saudi Arabia, however, also uses it as a daily, commercial calendar.

FYI FACT:

Private companies and banks are open every day but Friday, the Muslim holy day, when everything is closed. Government employees get a two-day weekend: Thursday and Friday.

In the sixteenth century, the Arabian Peninsula was part of the Ottoman Empire. The Turks were eventually driven out, and Abdul Aziz Al Saud, commonly called Ibn Saud, established the kingdom of Saudi Arabia in 1932. Only his descendants can legally rule the country. That same decade, the discovery of oil transformed Saudi Arabia and the entire peninsula, giving it significant economic leverage that grew as the world became ever more dependent on oil. The oil also made the Saud family among the wealthiest in the world.

Today, Saudi Arabia is a country whose rich history and natural beauty are often overlooked by much of the Western world, which finds the conservative Islamic culture's treatment of women and the Saud family's refusal to promote civil liberties unacceptable. At the same time, Saudi Arabia has been the United States' closest economic and political ally among Islamic countries.

While its oil revenue ensures a comfortable present, the world's efforts to eliminate its dependence on fossil fuels through renewable energies like wind and solar power, plus the eventual depletion of the country's oil reserves, leaves Saudi Arabia facing a precarious future. In a modern irony, the nomadic Bedouins, who still shepherd their flocks across the harsh landscape as their ancestors did thousands of years ago, may prove to be the best prepared to deal with the twenty-first-century goal of a global "green" environment.

WHERE IN THE WORLD IS SAUDI ARABIA?

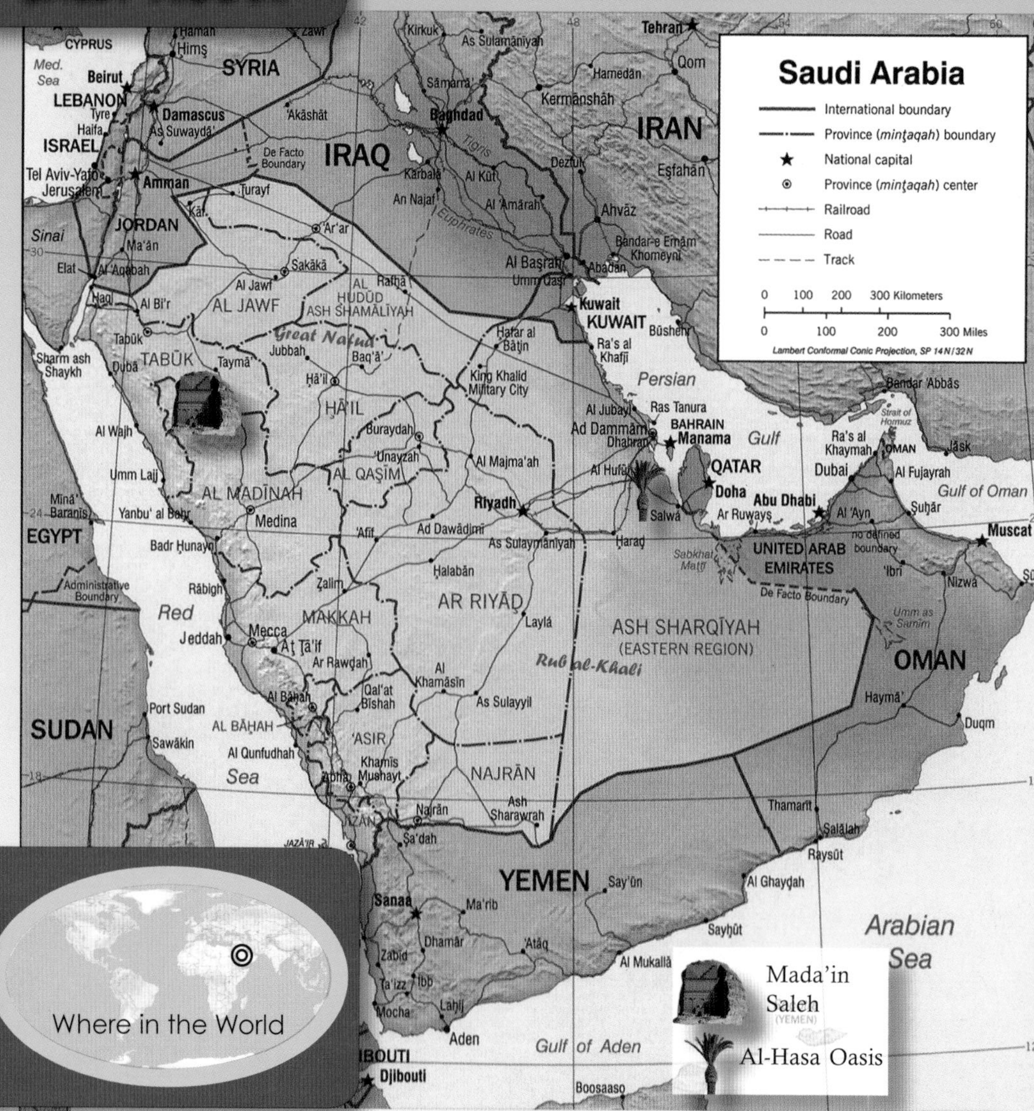

Saudi Arabia spans most of the Arabian Peninsula, between the Red Sea to the west and the Persian Gulf to the east. In the Arab world, the Persian Gulf is called the Arabian Gulf. The vast majority of Saudi Arabia is uninhabited.

SAUDI ARABIA FACTS AT A GLANCE

Falconry

Full country name: Kingdom of Saudi Arabia (Al Mamlakah al Arabiyah as Suudiyah)

Language: Arabic (Modern Standard Arabic)

Population: 28.6 million

Area: 830,000 square miles (2,149,690 square kilometers), roughly one third the size of the United States

Capital city: Riyadh

Largest cities: Riyadh (6.7 million), Jeddah (3.6 million), Mecca (1.7 million), and Medina and Dammam (1.3 million each)

Government: Absolute monarchy, with no written constitution; rule is based on Islamic law

Ethnic makeup: Arab (90 percent) and Afro-Asian (10 percent)

Religion: Islamic (95 percent Sunni Muslims; 5 percent Shi'ite Muslims)

Climate: Hot, although some northern regions can fall below freezing in winter

Average rainfall: 4 inches (10 centimeters) per year

Lowest point: Persian Gulf (sea level)

Highest point: Jabal Sawda' (10,279 feet/ 3,133 meters)

Popular sports: Falconry, Horse Racing, Soccer

National tree: Date palm (*Phoenix dactylifera*)

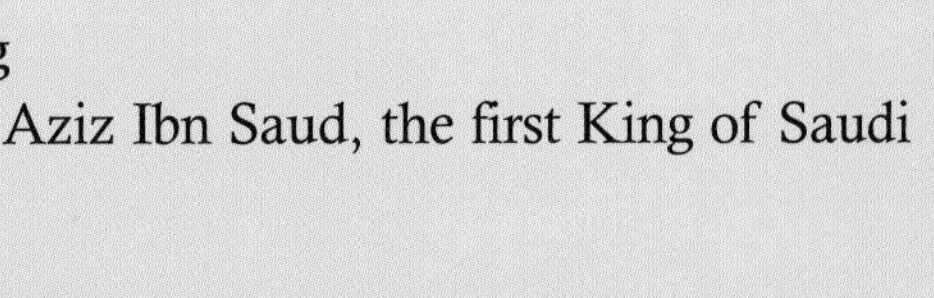

Flag: The flag of Saudi Arabia is green, the traditional color of Islam, with the inscription "There is no God but Allah and Muhammad is his Prophet" written in white Arabic script above a white sword. The flag was adopted on March 15, 1973, and the design was based on the flag that represented the army of Abdul Aziz Ibn Saud, the first King of Saudi Arabia.

Sources: *CIA World Factbook*, "Saudi Arabia"; U.S. Department of State, "Saudi Arabia"; "Pilgrimage to Karbala—Sunni and Shia: The Worlds of Islam," *Wide Angle*, March 26, 2007, http://www.pbs.org/wnet/wideangle/episodes/pilgrimage-to-karbala/sunni-and-shia-the-worlds-of-islam/1737/

Abdul Aziz Al Saud was the first monarch of Saudi Arabia. His full name was Abdul Aziz Ibn Abdul Rahman Al Faisal Ibn Saud, but he was most commonly known as Ibn Saud. He fathered over 50 children with his 22 wives, and as of 2011, every king of Saudi Arabia since his death has been one of his sons.

Chapter 2
A Brief History

Despite the inhospitable conditions found there, the Arabian Peninsula has been populated since around 8000 BCE.[1] Throughout much of that time, the peninsula remained a place of mystery. Historians know very little about these early Semitic hunter-gatherers, in part because many were nomadic and also because, compared to Egypt or other areas in the region, archaeologists have not explored it extensively. It is believed the earliest inhabitants migrated to the peninsula from the Levant—the part of the Fertile Crescent adjacent to the eastern end of the Mediterranean.

The southern end of the peninsula—the location of modern-day Yemen and Oman—gets the most rain, so it was likely settled first because it could sustain farming. Eventually kingdoms were established there. Historians believe that the Queen of Sheba, who is mentioned in the Bible, was a ruler from southern Arabia. Lush, tropical, and exotic, this was the land where a mythology filled with tales of jinns and genies, magic lamps and flying carpets developed and was passed down through generations.

The northern and eastern parts of the peninsula were too arid to sustain farming, so the Bedouins were nomadic by necessity. Usually on donkeys, they drove their sheep back and forth, up and down the peninsula, following available water. Since they moved around so much, some of these nomads became involved in trade, working as middlemen for goods passing from India to Egypt and back again.

Muslims call the time prior to Muhammad the Age of Ignorance. Until the emergence of Christianity, Arabs believed in many deities, just as the Romans and Greeks did. Three of the best known were goddesses. Manat was the goddess of rain, health, and destiny; Al-Lat—represented by a large, flat stone and smaller precious stones kept in a wooden box—protected travelers; and Al-Uzza was a love goddess. In addition, each tribe worshiped its own particular god. Muhammad's tribe, for example, worshiped a tree called Dhat Anwat that grew along the road connecting Mecca to Medina. Whereas the Greek gods united the various Greek city-states, the early Arab pantheon varied according to tribe.

Other factors separated Arabs as well, and by the time Jesus of Nazareth was born, the northern tribes had developed into two vastly different cultures. Their differences were similar to those seen between America's northern and southern states prior to the Civil War. The nomadic Bedouins were shepherds who lived in small tribes that were extremely close-knit. The sedentary Arabs were Bedouins involved in trade who chose to settle in the oases that line the edges of the Arabian Desert, along the land trade routes. Most of these settlements were not established until after 1000 BCE.

While the nomadic Bedouins were a peaceful people, the sedentary Arabs often used military force to protect the precious resources offered by the oases. They prospered through trade and as a result grew more powerful than their nomadic kin.

Over time, Christianity, and to a lesser degree Judaism, spread throughout the peninsula, but the religious and cultural landscape of Arabia changed forever in the early seventh century after Muhammad founded Islam. Over the next millennia, Islam would become the primary religion of the Middle East as well as a way of life for all the Arab tribes. Instead of a disconnected collection of tribes, Islam created a unified Muslim-Arab community, or *umma*. It is not surprising, then, that the founding of Saudi Arabia was fueled in large part by religion.

In the centuries after Muhammad, many foreign invaders vied for control of Arabia, and by the early 1500s, the Ottoman Empire had conquered most of the area. As the Empire's control ended, the peninsula began to divide into distinct principalities.

Saudi Arabia began to form in the central region of the peninsula after a local ruler, Muhammad Ibn Saud, teamed up with Islamic reformer Muhammad Ibn Abdul Wahhab to create a new political group with Islam as the foundation. Ibn Saud's ancestors had settled near what is today Riyadh in the early sixteenth century and controlled the nearby date groves. The small town that eventually sprang up was ruled by the Al Saud family.

Muhammad Ibn Saud and Al Wahhab wanted all the Arabs of the peninsula to adhere to Islam in its purest form. In 1744, they made a pact with each other to achieve their goal. In addition to their personal agreement, bin Saud's son, Abdul Aziz, married Al Wahhab's daughter, binding the two families with a commitment that lasts to this day.

Wahhabi leaders waged a jihad, or holy war, against other, less strict forms of Islam on the peninsula and succeeded in uniting most of Arabia. But by 1818, the Ottomans and their Egyptian allies drove out the Wahhabis.

In 1902, Abdul Aziz Al Saud, referred to as Ibn Saud, and his Wahhabi followers captured Riyadh and assumed the leadership of the Arab nationalist movement. Over the next three decades he systematically brought more and more of Arabia under his control, and in 1932 he officially established the kingdom of Saudi Arabia. That same decade saw the discovery of huge oil reserves, which made the Saud family massively rich and enabled them to stabilize their new country.

The country remains the world's leading producer of oil, but Saudi Arabia has faced internal unrest as conservative traditionalists clash with progressives who want to see more modernization. How the Saudi royal family juggles their past traditions with modern economic, social, and political realities will directly impact the Middle East and the world.

Saudi King Abdullah and U.S. President Barack Obama meet in 2010. The United States and Saudi Arabia have had close political and economic ties since the 1930s. Although relations were strained after the 9/11 terrorist attacks, Saudi Arabia remains a strategic ally, including against the war on terrorism.

In Hollywood movies depicting ancient Arabia, the local rulers are wealthy sultans who wear silk clothes, live in glittering palaces, and rule with absolute authority. While the clothes are different, that image is not all that far from reality.

Saudi Arabia is a monarchy governed by the strict Islamic laws of the Wahhabi sect, so there is no written constitution or legislature, and political parties are banned. The king rules over what is known as the Third Saudi State.

The First Saudi State began in 1744 when Muhammad Ibn Saud agreed to support the cause of Abdul Wahhab to purify Islam. It lasted until 1818 when the Turks of the Ottoman Empire, in collaboration with Egypt, invaded and conquered central Arabia.

The Second Saudi State was established beginning in 1824 when the Saud family regained power after Imam Turki Ibn Abdullah captured the city of Riyadh from the armies of Egyptian ruler Muhammad Ali Pasha. This dynasty lasted approximately 75 years, but in the end was weakened by infighting within the Saud family. In 1891, the forces of the last Saudi imam, Abdul Rahman Al Faisal, were defeated in the northern town of Ha'il by the army of their sworn enemies, the Al Rashid family, whose Baghdad dynasty had been the inspiration for *The Arabian Nights: Tales from a Thousand and One Nights*.

After the Rashidis conquered Riyadh, the Al Saud family was exiled to Kuwait, officially ending the Second Saudi State. Ten years later, Abdul Aziz, better known as Ibn Saud in the West, asked the Kuwaiti

Located in Riyadh, the Kingdom Center is the tallest skyscraper in Saudi Arabia and holds the highest mosque in the world. The center includes a five-level shopping mall, a Four Seasons hotel, and apartments.

emir for men and supplies to regain his homeland. Kuwait had also been at war with the Rashidis, so the prince agreed to supply Ibn Saud with weapons and soldiers.

In January 1902, Ibn Saud and his 68 men reached Riyadh. Unable to match the manpower of the Rashidis, Ibn Saud laid out a plan to capture Al Musmak Castle and kill the Rashidi leader in charge of Riyadh. His strategy worked, and within a day he had regained control of the city. This marked the beginning of the Third Saudi State.

Under the leadership of Ibn Saud, the Saudis reestablished their empire in central and eastern Arabia. To ensure they would not be overrun again by foreign invaders, Ibn Saud recruited town militias and also organized an army comprised of former nomads who were trained to be soldiers on behalf of Islam.

Ibn Saud first secured control of coastal eastern Arabia, a very poor region that would later become famous for its vast oil reserves. From 1924 to 1925, the Saudis, while expelling the Hashemite royal family from Mecca and Medina, took control of those cities. When the Kingdom of Saudi Arabia was officially founded in 1932, Ibn Saud made peace with his new country's neighbors and did not pursue any further armed expansion of Wahhabi Islam.

During and after World War II, oil revenues steadily increased, giving the Saud family unprecedented wealth, enabling them to improve the lives of their subjects by expanding education and building modern infrastructure so that more people could come live in the cities. All this was done in compliance with Islamic law as interpreted by the Wahhabi Sauds. The Koran (or Qur'an) remained the basis of the government and the political system. Respected Wahhabi religious scholars gave the Saud dynasty legitimacy, and in return, the Saudi kings maintained the state's official conservative religious values.

By 2010, there were approximately 22,000 members of the royal family, and they held the majority of the top positions in business, government, the military, and the judiciary. Since the death of King Abdul Aziz in 1953, succession in Saudi Arabia has passed, in order of seniority, to his sons. King Abdullah, who was born in 1924, has ruled since 2005.

In 1992 the Basic Law was adopted. According to the *CIA World Factbook*, it declared that "Saudi Arabia was a monarchy ruled by the sons and grandsons of King Abd Al Aziz Al Saud, and that the Holy Qur'an is the constitution of the country, which is governed on the basis of Islamic law (Shari'a). There are no political parties or national elections; however, the country held its first municipal elections in 2005. The king's powers are limited because he must observe the Shari'a and other Saudi traditions. He also must retain a consensus of the Saudi royal family, religious leaders (ulema), and other important elements in Saudi society. In the past the leading members of the royal family chose the king from among themselves with the subsequent approval of the ulema."[1]

Even though there is no legislature, by necessity the Saudi kings have gradually developed a central government to oversee the running of the country. Beginning in 1953, the king has appointed a Council of Ministers who act as advisers to help determine general policy. The council is made up of a prime minister, the first and second deputy prime ministers, twenty ministers, two ministers of state, plus a few advisers and heads of major autonomous organizations. All decisions must be compatible with Muhammad's teachings.

In October 2006, King Abdullah established the Allegiance Council in an attempt to build a consensus for choosing future crown princes and to settle potential succession disputes between rival factions of the royal family.

Just as religion formed the basis of their government, it also informed Saudi political foreign policy. For example, the government was against both Israel, a Jewish state, and the Soviet Union, an atheist state.

The Saudi monarchs use their vast wealth—in 2009, King Abdullah was worth an estimated $17 billion[2]—to promote the spread of Islam and to back various Muslim nations and groups, such as the World Muslim League, which promotes Islam, and the Organization of the Islamic Conference, a multinational association of Muslim countries that organizes conferences of government leaders.

Despite the country's extreme social conservatism when compared to most Western cultures, a segment of the Saudi population feels the royal family is too religiously liberal. Other than fundamentalist strongholds such as Iran, most of the Islamic countries slowly became more secular in the latter half of the twentieth century. Saudi Arabia, though, remained officially committed to promoting religion. Even so, some Muslims in Saudi Arabia accused the Saud dynasty of corruption and claimed there was a double standard because the numerous princes did not have to abide equally by sacred law. In November 1979, a group of fundamentalist Islamic militants seized control of the Ka'ba, the sacred cube located inside the Grand Mosque in Mecca. They demanded the overthrow of the Saud dynasty and a return to strict Islamic practices.

Saudi Arabia has also been criticized by some citizens and by some other Muslim countries for its relationship with the United States; specifically, relying on the U.S. military to protect Saudi Arabia from possible attacks from Iraq and Iran over the years. For example, during the Gulf War in 1991, when Iraq invaded Kuwait, U.S. and other United Nations troops were allowed to have a base camp in Saudi Arabia. The continued presence of American troops after the Gulf War ended outraged many fundamentalist Muslims—including the

When the Saudi government allowed the U.S. military to establish a base there during the Gulf War, many fundamentalist Muslims were angry.

scion of a wealthy Saudi family, Osama bin Laden. The primary reason given for the September 11, 2001, terrorist attacks on the United States was Bin Laden's anger over the presence of U.S. troops in Saudi Arabia. Many of the hijackers were Saudis. Later, it was discovered that members of the Saud family were supporting fundamentalist groups with terrorist ties, such as Hamas in Palestine and Hizb ut Tahrir in Central Asia. These revelations caused tension between the Saudi Arabian government and the United States.

But the monarchy was not immune from Bin Laden, either. In May and November of 2003, Bin Laden's group, al-Qaeda, incited riots and took credit for bombings in Riyadh. Religious leaders that support the monarchy issued fatwas, or religious edicts, that forbade suicide attacks and violence between Muslims. The bombings prompted Saudi Arabia to step up efforts against terrorism, and in February 2005, the Saudi government sponsored the first ever Counter-Terrorism International Conference in Riyadh. Saudi Arabia and the United States remain important allies in the war on terror.

Some of the dunes in the north-central area of the Rub al-Khali, or Empty Quarter, are made of red sand. The swirling desert winds create dunes in a variety of shapes and patterns.

The Arabian Desert is a vast expanse that stretches east to west from the Persian Gulf to Yemen, and north to south from Iraq to Oman. A desert is defined as a region that receives less than 10 inches (25 centimeters) of rain annually, but not all deserts are created equal, and how they look can vary dramatically. More than half the area of Saudi Arabia is desert.

In the northwest of Saudi Arabia is the Great Nafud desert, which covers 2,500 square miles (4,023 square kilometers), larger than the state of Delaware. Iron oxide in the sand gives it a unique reddish color. Enough rain falls in the winter to grow vegetation such as shrubs, wildflowers, and assorted herbs used for grazing by Bedouins.

In southern Saudi Arabia is Rub Al-Khali, which means Empty Quarter, the largest continuous sand desert in the world. Its 250,000-square-mile (402,000-square-kilometer) area—slightly smaller than Texas—covers more than a quarter of the country.[1] The region is extremely dry and virtually uninhabited but is valued for its oil reserves. There are sand dunes in Rub Al-Khali that tower hundreds of feet high, and the swirling wind moves the sand into strange shapes and patterns that have prompted some people to call the desert Mars on Earth. There are also areas of deadly quicksand. Temperatures higher than 120°F (48°C) are regularly recorded there. With all the sand, dust storms are a common hazard. There are only 37 plant species in the Empty Quarter, 17 of which are found on the periphery, with only one or two considered native. Compare that to the Mojave

Desert in the American West, which has over 200 endemic plant species.

However, after a period of rainfall, seeds that have lain dormant beneath the surface will grow and bloom within a matter of days. Visitors who have the fortune of being in the Arabian Desert after a rare rainfall will see sunflowers, wild irises, cornflowers, lavender, and other varieties turning the desert green for a brief time.

The central and northern parts of Saudi Arabia are mostly gravel plains that are hot and humid in the summer. However, northern regions can drop to below freezing in the winter. The eastern portion of the country is an area of low-lying salt flats that is home to the immense Al-Hasa Oasis, which is filled with date palms, the only significant flora, or plant life, in the area. The most unique area of Saudi Arabia is the grassland and tree-filled southern Asir region.

Saudi Arabia is so dry, there are no permanent rivers or lakes, but it has 1,640 miles (2,460 kilometers) of coastline. Along the Red Sea are coral reefs that are home to a diverse collection of marine life.

The miniata grouper, also known as the miniatus grouper, coral or blue-spot rockcod, coral hind, and coral grouper, lives along the coral reefs of the Indian Ocean.

Striped Hyena

By far the most common animal in Saudi Arabia is the dromedary (one-hump) camel, which has been domesticated for centuries, particularly by the Bedouin tribes. Because of the harsh environment, Saudi Arabia has limited indigenous wildlife. Ibex, baboons, wolves, wildcats, spiny-tailed lizards, snakes, and hyenas are native to the mountainous areas, while a variety of birds can be found in the oases. Because of overhunting and habitat destruction, many species have gone extinct, including the striped hyena, jackals, and honey badgers. Green sea turtles nest on the beaches along the Red Sea and Persian Gulf, but these animals also face threats from pollution and loss of inshore feeding grounds.

Baboons, however, have adapted remarkably well to the encroaching human population, and their numbers have increased. Baboons are a common sight on the mountain roads of southwestern Saudi Arabia, and many are not afraid of people. One reason for their thriving population is that their natural predators are either endangered or extinct. Visitors to the baboon areas are asked not to feed the baboons so that they will retain their natural behavior.

Baboon

The nomadic Bedouins use camels for a variety of purposes. They are used for travel, for trade, for food, for their hides, and even for their milk, which contains more proteins and fat than cow milk.

Chapter 5

The People of Saudi Arabia

Compared to many Western countries such as the United States and Great Britain, Saudi Arabia is not a particularly diverse, melting-pot kind of country. The vast majority of Saudis are ethnically Arab, with an estimated 10 percent of the natives Afro-Asian. There are close to six million foreign nationals from India, Pakistan, Bangladesh, Indonesia, and the Philippines, most of whom immigrated as religious pilgrims. There are fewer than 100,000 Westerners in Saudi Arabia. As Saudi Arabian cities continue to grow, more Bedouins are giving up their nomadic lifestyle and settling in urban areas. Even so, there are still significant numbers of traditional Bedouin shepherds who continue to migrate in search of grazing land for their flocks.

Arabic is the official language of Saudi Arabia and much of the Middle East. Almost 200 million people in more than 20 countries speak Arabic, which is also the language of the Koran. Somewhat surprisingly, English is widely spoken in business and is a mandatory second language taught in schools. Spoken Arabic varies from country to country, but in Saudi Arabia classical Arabic has remained the same for centuries—although there are differences between the dialects spoken in urban areas and those spoken in rural areas. The Riyadh area has a distinctive regional speech pattern called the Najdi dialect, considered to be one of the most recognizable accents within the Arabic language. Najdi Arabic is widely spoken in the desert regions of central and eastern Saudi Arabia. Urdu, Farsi, and Turkic are the most common languages among the foreign nationals.

Even as the country's clerics enforce harsh rules governing personal conduct, the government has sought to broaden educational opportunities for its growing population of young people, including women.

The structure of the educational system is a lot like that in the United States. Children attend nursery school starting at three years old. Primary education begins with kindergarten at five years old and continues for seven years. To move on to the next level, students must pass a test at the end of seventh grade to get their Elementary Education Certificate. Intermediate education in Saudi Arabia, equivalent to middle school, lasts three years, as does secondary education, or high school. Boys and girls are segregated into separate, same-sex schools.

The first government school for girls was built in 1964; now there are girls' schools in every part of the country. By 2004, half of the 5 million students enrolled in Saudi schools were female. There are eleven government universities in Saudi Arabia, six for women. Former King Fahd encouraged women to take a more active role in public life, and Saudi women have been making inroads in professions such as teaching, medicine, and social work—professions where they do not have to have contact with men. Women are prohibited from certain careers such

Women are supposed to be covered in public. In advertisements, the printer distorts their faces to hide them.

as engineering, journalism, and architecture.

Although women cannot practice law in Saudi Arabia, in February 2010, the government announced it was drafting new rules to permit female lawyers to represent women in marriage, divorce, custody, and other family cases. Because Islamic law calls for the segregation of the genders, female lawyers can only work in places where they will not come into contact with men. All judges in the kingdom are male religious clerics.

FYI FACT:

Muslims use miswak, a twig from the arak tree, to clean their teeth.

Interestingly, Bedouin women enjoy greater freedom of dress and activity than their urban counterparts. For example, in rural areas, women may drive the tribe's water truck. In the city, however, women are prohibited from driving.

Veiling is a Bedouin tradition that dates back many centuries. Veils can be used for modesty but are also used for certain ceremonies and as a sign of respect when in the presence of authority figures. Many veils are extremely ornate and fashionable.

Carpentry, called Al-Nijarah, is one of the oldest artisan traditions of Saudi Arabia. Saudi carpenters are especially known for their decorative door and window shutters, designed with geometric patterns.

Chapter 6

Culture and Lifestyle

Saudi Arabia has a rich cultural history, but its modern culture is admittedly restrictive by Western standards. For example, alcohol, nightclubs, and movie theaters are prohibited. Soccer, however, is permitted. Riyadh has four soccer clubs and several stadiums.

While Saudis enjoy music—especially Western music among the young—playing music and dancing in public is generally not permitted. Venues where musicians just get together and play are simply not available.

A Coca-Cola can

There are many traditional folk dances, but again, occasions and places to perform them are limited. The national dance of Saudi Arabia is the men's sword dance called the *ardh*. Men in traditional clothing carry a sword as they move in time to the music. The sword dance originated in the Najd region of Saudi Arabia and is one of the oldest forms of dance.

For whatever they lack in outside diversion, Saudis make up for with other activities. They love eating at restaurants, and city visitors can choose from a wide selection of Asian, American, and

Iranian restaurants. Fast-food chains such as McDonald's and KFC have become increasingly popular in the country. Coffee shops are also especially popular.

One of the favorite national pastimes in urban areas is shopping, with many Western-style malls available. Don't be afraid to bargain—it is part of the culture.

When visiting Saudi Arabia, it is very important to be mindful of local customs and etiquette. Traveling to another country can give you a chance to see daily life from a different perspective, which will help you to understand their lifestyle choices. For example, all Muslims are required to pray five times a day: dawn, noon, afternoon, sunset, and evening. The exact prayer times are listed in the local newspaper each day. At those times, people stop what they are doing, face Mecca, and pray. Visitors to Saudi Arabia are expected to do the same. Saudis don't expect as much personal space as Westerners do; they may stand closer than you are used to.

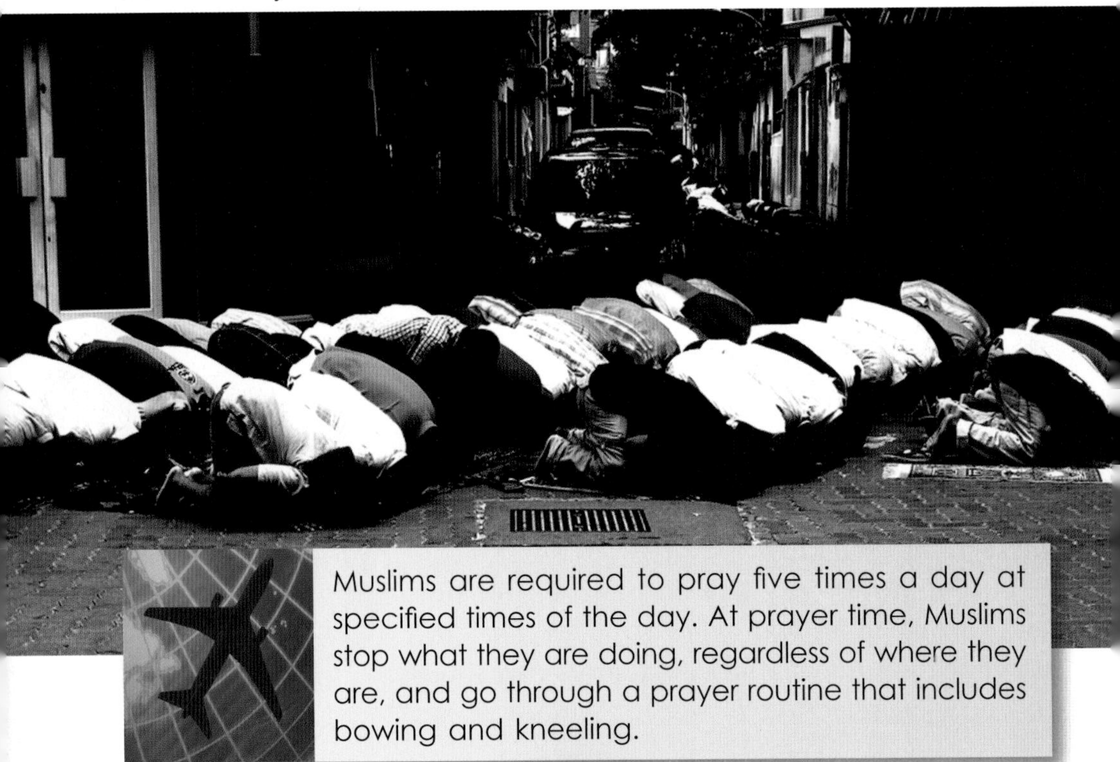

Muslims are required to pray five times a day at specified times of the day. At prayer time, Muslims stop what they are doing, regardless of where they are, and go through a prayer routine that includes bowing and kneeling.

FYI FACT:

Equestrian Dalma Rushdi Malhas, then eighteen, was the first Saudi woman to participate in any Olympic-branded competition when she competed at the first Youth Olympic Games, held August 2010 in Singapore. It was also the first time a Saudi woman athlete officially represented the Kingdom at an international competition. Malhas, and her horse Flash Top Hat, earned a bronze medal in the individual show jumping event. Malhas' medal was Saudi Arabia's third in an Olympic competition. Fellow equestrian Khalid Al-Eid won a bronze and hurdler Hadi Souan Somayli won a silver in the 2000 Sydney Games.

Dalma Malhas

Non-Saudi or non-Muslim men and women are not expected to wear Arab garments, but they must dress modestly. Taking the time to learn some basic Arabic phrases of how to greet people will be appreciated and well received. If you are invited to a Saudi's house, it is proper to bring a small gift. However, gifts are not opened when received.

It is traditional for men and women to be segregated into different rooms during dinner. Always be gracious and accept the offer of Arabian coffee and dates. Called *gahwa*, the ritual of serving coffee to visitors is an old tradition and is very important to Saudis.

It is common to eat while sitting on the floor, so keep your body compact, either sitting cross-legged or kneeling on one knee. Eat only with the right hand out of respect because in Islam, the left hand is unclean. While there is a lot of conversation before and after meals, dinner itself is usually eaten in silence so that the food can be fully appreciated.

Segregation between men and women is usually strictly enforced in Saudi restaurants, in large part because eating requires removal of the veil. Most restaurants have family and single (or male only) sections. Women who are not accompanied by their husbands or a male relative are usually not allowed in.

Chicken Bukhari is a popular Saudi Arabian dish. It was brought to the Middle East from Central Asia by Muslim pilgrims who came to Mecca. The dish is made with rice, tomatoes, watercress, onions, hot tomato sauce, and grilled chicken.

While there are some Islamic dietary restrictions—according to the Koran, pork is impure—Saudi Arabian cuisine is flavorful and varies, with traditional dishes that contain meat, rice, wheat, vegetables, and spices. One of Saudi Arabia's famous dishes is Al-Kabsa, which is made of rice cooked with lamb or chicken in a pot. Beef is very rare in the Middle East.

Some cooking traditions are centuries old. A popular way of preparing meat is called Al-Mandi, for which a lamb or chicken is barbecued in a deep hole in the ground. Meat is also prepared by grilling it on flat stones that are placed on top of burning embers. Along the coastal areas, dishes often contain seafood.

In addition to becoming familiar with the customs, it is also important for visitors to be aware of local laws. Women are not allowed to drive, and men are prohibited from being with women they are not related to (including girlfriends). Drinking alcohol, dressing immodestly, and blasphemy are also unlawful. In Saudi Arabia, religious police officers called Mutawwa'in enforce these rules, and ignorance of the law is not accepted as an excuse.

Saudi Arabia is the world's leading producer of oil. The kingdom's first commercial oil field was discovered near Dhahran in 1931. By 2010, the vast majority of the Saudi workforce was employed by the oil industry.

Chapter 7

Saudi Economy and Commerce

Oil . . . oil . . . and more oil—and some dates—are the backbone of the Saudi economy.

Saudi Arabia is the world's leading exporter of oil, which accounts for an estimated 80 percent of the country's wealth. That wealth is concentrated mostly in the royal family—the annual per capita income is under $15,000 a year.[1]

Unemployment is a growing problem among Saudi nationals, especially among the large youth population, which lacks the technical skills and education to work at hi-tech jobs. Close to six million foreign workers fill those positions in the oil and service industries.[2] In an effort to get their young people needed training, the King Abdullah University of Science and Technology—Saudi Arabia's first coeducational university—opened in Riyadh in September 2009.[3]

With the world working to reduce or eliminate its dependence on fossil fuels in favor of clean, renewable energy such as wind and solar power, the Saudi Arabian government is working hard to shore up other industries, which include steel, dates, pharmaceuticals, and

Date tree

Picnicking in the Arabian Desert is a favorite pastime for locals and tourists. One of the more novel customs is buying from the fleet of ice cream trucks that travels to the desert to serve the picnickers.

plastics. The country also has mineral deposits that include gold, iron ore, copper, phosphates, and bauxite.

Most of the land is not suitable for farming, but while agriculture is a minor industry overall, it produces significant numbers of sheep, dates, and grain. The growing population and expanding cities have brought many construction jobs, most of which are funded by the government.

One of the biggest issues facing Saudi Arabia is the lack of fresh drinking water. The solution has been desalination technology, which turns seawater into drinking water by taking out the salt and other impurities. Saudi Arabia currently produces about 18 percent of the world's desalinated water. In 2010, the government announced plans to build the first water desalination plant powered by solar energy. The goals of the project are to create stable power and water supplies in Saudi Arabia for future generations.

The government is trying to establish a better tourist trade, especially ecotourism for such areas as the Empty Quarter and the coral reefs in the Gulf of Aqaba. While the country has areas of great historical interest, the social restrictions of Islamic law have kept away many Westerners. For the same reasons, Saudi Arabia is not a popular destination among many Arabs in neighboring Middle Eastern countries. The notable exception is the Hajj, but in that case, the visitors are there for a religious experience, not to travel and spend money.

In an effort to give its country a broader international appeal, the Saudi government announced plans in April 2010 to build the largest ecotourism park in the Middle East. Musma Park will be located in the northwestern Ha'il Province to promote desert tourism.[4]

The government also announced plans to build a $13.32 billion tourist city in the eastern beach city of Al-Oqair that will have a performance stage, a heritage village, and a site for fireworks. Whether or not the tourist city will be exempt from some of the social restrictions found in the rest of Saudi Arabia was not disclosed.

FYI FACT:

Gold was first mined in Saudi Arabia 3,000 years ago. Some archaeologists believe a huge deserted gold mine found between Mecca and Medina belonged to King Solomon, who is listed on the Forbes list of Top Ten Wealthiest Historical Figures.

In the U.S. Supreme Court Building is a frieze depicting Muhammad and many other great figures in history. After the image of the prophet provoked controversy, the Supreme Court included this statement in tourist materials: "The figure is a well-intentioned attempt by the sculptor to honor Muhammad, and it bears no resemblance to Muhammad. Muslims generally have a strong aversion to sculptured or pictured representations of their Prophet."[1]

Because Saudi Arabia was founded as an Islamic state, it is not surprising that the majority of its most famous people are associated in some way with religion; none more so than Muhammad, the most famous Saudi of all.

The Messenger of God

To Muslims, Muhammad is seen as the last of God's great prophets, which include Jesus and Moses. Muhammad was born around 570 CE in Mecca. His father had died before his birth and his mother died when he was six. He lived with his grandfather; then, after his grandfather's death, he went to live with his uncle, who raised him. Having no family inheritance, Muhammad grew up without wealth.

Sometime around 595, a wealthy widow named Khadija hired Muhammad to travel to Syria as the steward, or protector, of her trading supplies. Later, Muhammad married her and together they had four daughters; none of their sons lived past infancy.

Now financially secure, Muhammad began to reflect on the paganism being practiced in Mecca and the lack of religious unity. One day around 610, when Muhammad was meditating, he heard a voice tell him he was the messenger of God. He later decided it had been the angel Gabriel. After more meditation and talking it over with friends, he became convinced he was being called to spread the message of God to the Arabs, just as Moses had done for Jews and Jesus had done for Christians.

He continued to receive messages for the rest of his life, which he collected into the chapters that make up the Koran. Muslims believe the words in the Koran came directly from God.

Initially, Muhammad shared these messages only with friends, but beginning around 612 he began preaching them publicly. He gained many followers but he also gained adversaries, especially among the leading merchants of Mecca. In September 622, Muhammad settled in the area of Medina, two hundred miles north of Mecca, along with a group of his followers. This led to a conflict between Muhammad's followers and Meccans. The fighting ended in 628 with the Treaty of al-Hudaybiya. Muhammad could now preach in peace, and the number of his followers kept growing. So did the number of his wives, which stood at nine. By 630, Muhammad had returned to Mecca with thousands of followers, and Islam became firmly rooted in his hometown.

Muhammad's greatest political achievement was using Islam to unite the different Arab tribes within an Islamic-based empire. At the time of his death in 632, Muhammad controlled a majority of Arabia.

Muhammad bin Abdul-Wahhab

Muhammad bin Abdul-Wahhab is arguably the second most important religious figure in Saudi Arabian history. He was born in 1703 in Uyaynah, an oasis village in Najd, the central region of Saudi Arabia, located around 18 miles (30 kilometers) from modern Riyadh. His father was a scholar, and Wahhab inherited a love of learning. By the time he was ten he had memorized the Koran. When he was older he went to study in Medina and also traveled to Iraq and Iran. In the late 1730s he returned to Najd, where many people still practiced polytheism.

Upset at the rampant paganism, as well as by Muslims who he felt were not properly following their faith, Wahhab became a religious activist. Preaching that there is only one God, he intended to return Islam to what he deemed was its purest form. His followers called themselves *muwahhidun*, which translates to "unitarians." Detractors called them Wahhabis.

Wahhab died in 1792, but through his pact with Muhammad ibn Saud to establish a country based on Islamic principles, Wahhabism eventually became Saudi Arabia's dominant religion. It is a very conservative form of Islam that believes in a literal interpretation of the Koran, much as Creationists believe in a literal interpretation of the Bible. Strict Wahhabis consider anyone who does not believe in their form of religion an enemy. Critics claim that Wahhabism actually misinterprets Islam and promotes intolerance, leading to extremist groups such as al-Qaeda. Although Wahhabism is the dominant sect in Saudi Arabia, it is a minority sect within the whole of Islam.

Osama bin Laden

One of the most admired men by radical fundamentalist Muslims is also the most wanted man by the United States government. Osama bin Laden has been a polarizing figure ever since he became a household name after the September 11, 2001, terrorist attacks on the World Trade Center in New York City and the Pentagon in Washington, D.C. He is also suspected of masterminding the 1993 bombing of the World Trade Center and the suicide bombing of the U.S. warship *Cole* in 2000, among other attacks around the world.

Bin Laden was born in Riyadh around 1957 to one of Saudi Arabia's wealthiest families. He had over 50 siblings—polygamy is allowed under Islamic law, and a man may take up to four wives.

Bin Laden earned a civil engineering degree at King Abdul Aziz University, but after the Soviet Union invaded Afghanistan in 1979, bin Laden, along with thousands of other Muslims from the Middle East, joined the Afghan resistance (the mujahideen). He believed it was his Muslim duty to fight against the

Osama bin Laden

occupation of an Islamic country. Ironically, during this time he worked with U.S. officials to end the Soviet occupation. But by 1988 he had already established al-Qaeda, Arabic for "the Base." It was a network of like-minded militant Muslims bin Laden knew from Afghanistan.

After the Soviets pulled out of Afghanistan in 1989, bin Laden returned to Saudi Arabia as a hero. He was dismayed by what he found at home: The Saudi government, he believed, and his own family, were corrupt. His biggest upset was over the presence of U.S. troops in Saudi Arabia during the 1991 Persian Gulf War. Now al-Qaeda saw themselves as holy warriors in a battle against the American infidels.

Al-Qaeda organized and carried out many attacks worldwide, targeting Americans or American interests in Egypt, Saudi Arabia, Kenya, and Tanzania.[2] By 1993, more than 200 people had died in the attacks. According to the 9/11 Commission Report, bin Laden went to Sudan in 1992 where he taught militants terrorist methods. In 1994, the Saudi government accused him of subversion and revoked his passport, essentially stripping him of his citizenship. His family was also pressured into cutting him off financially. The Sudanese government eventually made bin Laden leave in 1996, and he found refuge in Afghanistan, under the ruling Taliban militia.

Between 1996 and 1998, bin Laden issued several fatwas declaring a holy war against the United States. He charged the United States with looting the natural resources of the Muslim world and helping the enemies of Islam (meaning Israel). It is believed bin Laden wanted to push the United States into a wide-scale war that would overthrow the moderate Muslim governments so that they could be replaced

FYI FACT:

Prince Sultan Ibn Salman became the first Arab and first Muslim to travel in space. He rode aboard the space shuttle *Discovery* in 1985.

by one large, fundamentalist Islamic state—something the majority of Muslims did not want.[3]

After the September 11 attacks, a coalition army led by the United States overthrew the Taliban in Afghanistan and forced bin Laden into hiding. It is believed he remained holed up in the remote, inaccessible mountainous terrain along the Afghanistan-Pakistan border, but the actual whereabouts of bin Laden has remained a mystery. The U.S. Department of State offered a standing reward of $25 million for information leading directly to bin Laden's capture or conviction.

Nimah Nawwab

Born in Malaysia to a Meccan family, Nimah Nawwab has become an internationally recognized literary figure and the first Saudi female poet to be published in the United States. Her father was a scholar, and Nimah became interested in English literature as a young girl and graduated from college with a bachelor of arts degree in English literature. Since then, her web site says Nimah has worked to build bridges of understanding. As a result, she is considered a cultural ambassadress and a voice for Arab women.[4]

Her articles and essays about Saudi society, customs, and Islam have been published throughout the Middle East and beyond. She has been a regular story and photography contributor to *Saudi Aramco World* magazine since the late 1990s. And her book of poetry, *The Unfurling*, which addresses issues of freedom, women, family, culture, faith, tradition, and tolerance, was published in 2004.

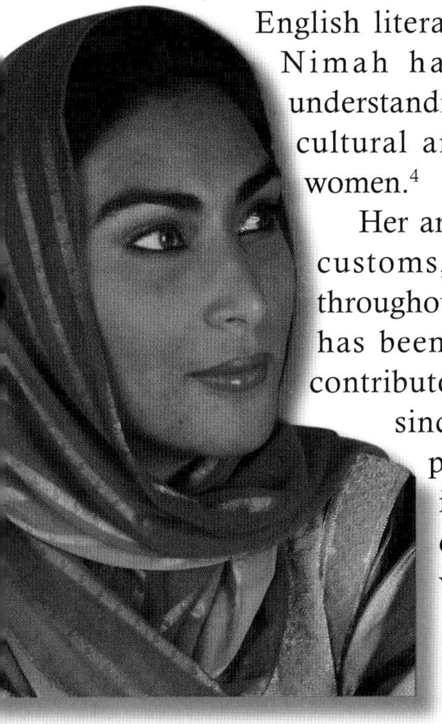

Nimah Nawwab

The Hawks of the Royal Saudi Air Force perform aerial maneuvers. Saudi Arabia has a relatively small military. However, it makes up for its lack of size by relying on state-of-the-art technology. Many of the aircraft used by the Royal Saudi Air Force come from the United States.

Because its government is based on the Koran, the national holidays were strictly religion-based until 2005, with Eid al-Adha and Eid al-Fitr being the only official holidays. Shortly after Abdullah bin Abdul Aziz became king, he established the first secular holiday, National Day, which celebrates the 1932 founding of Saudi Arabia.

Eid al-Adha, the Feast of Sacrifice, is observed at the end of the annual Hajj, which is the yearly pilgrimage to Mecca. According to Islamic law, Muslims must make the pilgrimage at least once in their life, unless prevented by some physical or financial hardship. During the Hajj, all Saudi government offices are closed, usually for 10 to 14 days.

The Hajj is a show of Muslim solidarity and submission to Allah (God). It begins on the eighth day of Dul-Hijjah, the twelfth month of the Islamic calendar. Hajj is associated with Abraham, called Ibrahim in Arabic. Three to five million Muslims gather in Mecca to perform a series of rituals commemorating the pilgrimage of Ibrahim and his son Ismail. Hajj consists of many rituals and prayers both at Masjid-al-Haram (The Holy Mosque) and locations around Mecca with religious significance, such as the Plain of Arafat.

Muslims consider Masjid al-Haram, which can accommodate more than 800,000 people, to be the holiest mosque in the world because it contains the Ka'ba, a black cube believed to have been built by Ibrahim and Ismail. Muslims believe the Ka'ba is located at the first place on

All Muslims are required to make the pilgrimage to Mecca at least once in their lives during the Hajj. In 2010 an estimated three million Muslims traveled to Mecca. The Masjid-al-Haram mosque can accommodate 800,000 people.

earth that Allah created. When Muslims face Mecca to pray, they are actually focusing on the Ka'ba, which enshrines a sacred stone.

Eid al-Adha is celebrated on the tenth day of Dul-Hajj. In most places, the Eid al-Adha celebration lasts several days. The exact dates of the feast vary, because Islamic months begin at sunset on the day when the lunar crescent first appears after the new moon, and can be seen with the naked eye. However, visibility depends on unpredictable factors such as weather conditions, so Eid al-Adha has typically been celebrated on different days in various areas of the world. Also, because Islamic dates are determined by a lunar calendar, the Feast of Sacrifice is observed about 11 days earlier each subsequent year.

The month of Ramadan is a time of personal reflection, spiritual renewal, and strict fasting—eating and drinking are prohibited during the daylight hours during Ramadan but are allowed after nightfall. At the end of Ramadan, Muslims observe an exuberant three-day celebration called Eid al-Fitr, the Festival of Fast-Breaking.

Before the start of Eid, each Muslim family gives a donation of food to the poor, such as rice, barley, and dates, to ensure that even

FYI FACT:

In 1853, British explorer Sir Richard Burton disguised himself as an Afghani Muslim to visit Mecca. The book *Personal Narrative of a Pilgrimage to Al-Madinah and Meccah* recounts his experience.

Muslims in need can have a holiday meal and participate in the celebration. This charitable donation is known as Sadaqa-ul-Fitr, "charity of fast-breaking."

Eid al-Fitr falls on the first day of Shawwal, the month after Ramadan. In the morning, Muslims gather early in outdoor locations or mosques to perform the Eid prayer, which is a sermon followed by a short congregational prayer. After the prayer is finished, everyone leaves to visit family and friends. It is common to bring gifts, especially to children. The celebration traditionally continues for three days.

Conservative clerics have denounced the secular celebrations associated with National Saudi Day, maintaining the only proper holidays are Islamic. But young Saudis in particular take to the streets because it is one of the few times public displays of nationalism are permitted. They drive around playing music and waving flags. In the evening there are many cultural events and fireworks displays. The festivities have proved so popular that each year more events are planned, to the dismay of the hard-line clerics.

Unofficial secular holidays such as Valentine's Day are strictly controlled; so much so that the exchange of flowers is banned, as is selling any red gifts in the days leading up to February 14. The restrictions have led to a black market for such items. The news agency AFP reported in 2009 how vendors secretly meet with customers in the middle of the night to sell a dozen red roses.[1] Islamic clerics believe Valentine's Day encourages premarital relations, which are illegal in the country and punishable by public whipping.[2]

Al Musmak Castle, built during the reign of Mohammed bin Abdullah bin Rashid, was captured by King Abdul Aziz in 1902. It features four watchtowers, a sitting room, a mosque, and a large open courtyard. The castle opened as a museum in 1995.

Mecca, the Saudi city with the richest history, and Medina are off limits to non-Muslims. For Muslims, these cities are places for praying, not sightseeing. However, other cities welcome tourists as long as they abide by local customs. For example, at many places around Riyadh, men and women cannot visit the same attraction on the same day; certain days are set aside for male visitors, other days for females.

Riyadh, the country's capital, is the largest city in Saudi Arabia. It is a modern city that keeps close ties with its past. Among the attractions is Al Musmak Castle, one of the most important landmarks in the kingdom because it is associated with Ibn Saud's conquest of the city and subsequent founding of the kingdom. The King Abdulaziz Center honors the one hundredth anniversary of Riyadh's recapture by Ibn Saud. The center was built to reflect the peninsula's culture and the message of Islam.

The National Museum offers visitors an excellent overview of the history and noteworthy sites of Saudi Arabia. Al Murabba'a Palace is located outside the city's walls and has been preserved to offer a glimpse into how Arabian royalty once lived.

Shopping is a main pastime, and there is a lot of it in Riyadh, both in traditional *souqs* (markets) and ultra-modern malls. A particularly fun shopping experience is the Camel Souq, where animals are bought and sold or traded. Most of the camel sellers do not mind having photos taken, but it is a good idea to ask first. Some Saudis object to photographs.

Snorkeling is a popular activity among visitors to Saudi Arabia. The waters near Jeddah are known for their coral reefs and the colorful variety of fish that live there.

Jeddah is located on the Red Sea, on the western side of Saudi Arabia. With its large percentage of foreign residents, it is a diverse city. The local religious culture is also less conservative than what is found in Riyadh. Old Jeddah is enclosed within walls and is a step back to when Jeddah was a dusty Arab village. In addition to a vibrant *souq*, Jeddah's Red Sea provides snorkeling, swimming, and diving, especially around the coral reefs.

To truly step back in time, visit the archaeological site at Mada'in Saleh. The ruins are from the Nabataeans, a tribe of Arabs who lived in the area around 2,000 years ago. Petra, located in modern Jordan,

FYI FACT:

The King Fahd Causeway that connects Saudi Arabia with Bahrain is 15.5 miles (24.9 kilometers) long, making it one of the longest causeways in the world.

was the capital of the Nabataean kingdom. The Nabataeans held a monopoly on the trade of incense and spices between the Far East and the Roman and Egyptian empires, and they became very wealthy because of it. There are over 130 tombs and dwellings spread out over an 8-mile (13-kilometer) area.

Al-Hasa Oasis, located 40 miles (64 kilometers) west of the Arabian Gulf, is a collection of many small towns, villages, and—according to locals—three million date palms. On one side is the ad-Dahna desert, on another the ad-Daman desert. Al-Hasa is one of the few agricultural areas, producing corn, citrus, rice, and lots and lots of dates. A constant problem facing Al-Hasa is encroaching sand, blown in from the deserts. To protect the oasis, the Saudi government has planted barriers of trees to keep the sand at bay.

Whether you tour Saudi Arabia's dynamic cities, hot deserts, tropical oases, or rocky mountains, you are sure to return home with a unique and memorable experience. Just imagine telling your family and friends about learning how Saudi Arabians eat, work, worship, and entertain themselves and others. They'll be thrilled to hear your stories!

Mada'in Saleh is an ancient archaeological site located in northwestern Saudi Arabia. It is known for its well-preserved tombs.

Saudi Date Sweet

Dates are one of the most popular fruits in the Middle East, dating back 6,000 years. Here is a recipe for a popular dessert made with dates. **Ask an adult to help you.**

- 4 tablespoons unsalted butter
- ½ cup walnuts, chopped
- ½ teaspoon cardamom, ground
- 1½ teaspoons brown sugar
- 1½ cups soft dates, pitted and chopped
- ¼ cup all-purpose flour

1. On medium heat, melt butter in a 9-inch skillet. Add walnuts and stir until lightly toasted.
2. Add cardamom, brown sugar, soft dates, and flour.
3. With a wooden spoon, mix until nuts and dates are covered. Remove from heat.
4. When the mixture has cooled, place your hand in a plastic bag and shape the sweets into balls the size of walnuts. Serve.

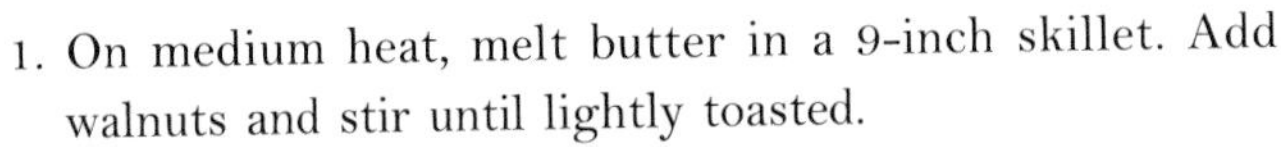

Jiffy Punch

- 12 ounces frozen orange juice concentrate
- 2 cups water
- Ice cubes
- 1 quart carbonated lemon-lime beverage, such as 7-Up (cold)
- 1 (8- to 12-ounce) package frozen strawberries
- Mint leaves or lime slices (optional)

1. In a punchbowl, combine orange juice and water; mix well.
2. Add ice cubes, then lemon-lime soda.
3. Puree strawberries and add, stirring to mix.
4. Garnish with mint and lime slices.

The Feast of Eid al-Fitr

Most Muslims include dates in the feasts they enjoy during the Eid al-Fitr festival at the end of the holy month of Ramadan. Create a display that represents the feast of Eid al-Fitr.

Materials:
Colored pencils
School glue
Scissors
File folders

Instructions:
1. Cut a file folder into a square.
2. Fold the square into a triangle; then fold it again to make a smaller triangle.
3. Open the file folder and cut along one of the new folds from the edge into the center of the square. Slide the two triangles on either side of the cut on top of one another to form a floor and two-sided corner.
4. Draw a picture of a dining room, with a table of food including dates. Add people and other decorations as you like, such as a Persian rug. Draw a picture of a date palm on another pice of file folder, cut it out, and add it to the display.
5. Pop up your three-sided diorama. Glue the bottom triangles to make the floor.

570	Muhammad is born.
630	Muhammad returns to Mecca in triumph.
1400s	Saudi dynasty is founded in the region around today's Riyadh.
1517	Ottomans gain control of the Arabian peninsula.
1744	First Saudi State is established.
1802	The Wahhabis conquer Mecca.
1812	The local population drives the Wahhabis out of Mecca.
1818	Wahhabis and Saudis found their capital in Riyadh.
1824	Second Saudi State begins.
1891	The Rashidi family exiles the Al Saud family to Kuwait.
1902	Ibn Saud regains control of Riyadh on January 15, starting the Third Saudi State. In June, he succeeds his father as leader of Al Saud.
1932	Saudi Arabia is founded on September 23.
1938	Oil is discovered in Dammam, near Dhahran, Saudi Arabia.
1940	Saudi Arabia is neutral during World War II until 1945 when it sides with the Allies against Germany.
1953	King Abdul Aziz dies November 9 and is succeeded by his son Saud.
1960	Saudi Arabia helps establish OPEC (Organization of Petroleum Exporting Countries).
1964	Prince Faisal replaces Saud as king and establishes a new political system.
1973	Saudi Arabia leads oil embargo against Western countries that support Israel.
1975	King Faisal is murdered by a nephew. He is succeeded by Khalid.
1982	King Khalid dies and is succeeded by King Fahd.
1990	Saudi Arabia condemns Iraq's invasion of Kuwait and asks the U.S. to intervene.
1991	Saudi Arabia participates in the Persian Gulf War against Iraq.
1994	Osama bin Laden is stripped of his Saudi citizenship.
2001	On September 11, Osama bin Laden launches terrorist attacks on the United States.
2005	King Fahd dies and is succeeded by Abdullah.
2009	Saudi officials arrest 44 suspected militants with links to Al-Qaeda.
2010	In London, the arrest of Prince Saud Abdulaziz bin Nasser al Saud for the murder of his servant brings to light class inequality in Saudi Arabia. Saudi Arabia donates over $100 million to flood victims in Pakistan.
2011	Saudi Arabia pledges $500 million to the Arab League fund, which supports small and medium start-up businesses and creates jobs for citizens in Arab countries. While King Abdullah recovers from surgery in Morocco, Crown Prince Sultan governs the kingdom.

Introduction

1. Alfred T. Mahan, "The Persian Gulf and International Relations," *The National Review*, September 1902, pp. 38–39; The Carolina Center for the Study of the Middle East and Muslim Civilizations, "Where Is the Middle East?" http://www.unc.edu/mideast/where/mahan-1902.shtml
2. Valentine Chirol, *The Middle Eastern Question, or Some Political Problems of Indian Defense* (London: John Murray, 1903), p. 5; The Carolina Center for the Study of the Middle East and Muslim Civilizations, "Where Is the Middle East?" http://www.unc.edu/mideast/where/chirol-1903.shtml

Chapter 1. Country Overview

1. CIA, The World Factbook: "Saudi Arabia," https://www.cia.gov/library/publications/the-world-factbook/geos/sa.html

Chapter 2. A Brief History

1. Drusilla Dunjie Houston, *Wonderful Ethiopians of the Ancient Cushite Empire* (Forgotten Books, 1926), online at http://www.sacred-texts.com/afr/we/index.htm

Chapter 3. Politics and Government

1. CIA World Factbook, Saudi Arabia https://www.cia.gov/library/publications/the-world-factbook/geos/sa.html
2. Tatiana Serafin, "The World's Richest Royals," *Forbes*, June 17, 2009. http://www.forbes.com/2009/06/17/monarchs-wealth-scandal-business-billionaires-richest-royals.html

Chapter 4. The Land

1. Rob Bowden, *Asia* (New York: Gareth Stevens, 2005).

Chapter 7. Saudi Economy and Commerce

1. U.S. Department of Commerce, International Trade Administration, "Saudi Arabia," Market of the Month, http://www.trade.gov/press/publications/newsletters/ita_0307/saudi_arabia_0307.asp
2. CIA World Factbook, Saudi Arabia, https://www.cia.gov/library/publications/the-world-factbook/geos/sa.html
3. Larry Abramson, "Saudi School Aims to Save the Planet," NPR, May 4, 2010, http://www.npr.org/templates/story/story.php?storyId=126484992
4. The White House, "April 1 – April 29, 2010: Hub Activities Report," http://www.whitehouse.gov/sites/default/files/microsites/ostp/04292010-newsletter.pdf

Chapter 8. Famous Saudi Arabians

1. Joan Biskupic, "Great Figures Gaze Upon the Court," *The Daily Republican*, March 11, 1998, http://www.dailyrepublican.com/sup_crt_frieze.html
2. Center for Defense Information: "Spotlight: Al Qaeda," *CDI Terrorism Project*, December 30, 2002, http://www.cdi.org/terrorism/alqaeda.cfm
3. Lisa Beyer, "Osama's End Game," *Time*, October 15, 2001, http://www.time.com/time/magazine/article/0,9171,1101011015-178412,00.html
4. Nimah Nawwab, "About Nimah I. Nawwab," http://www.nimahnawwab.com/about_nimah.html

Chapter 9. Saudi Festivals

1. "No Love for Valentines in Saudi Arabia," AFP, February 13, 2008, http://afp.google.com/article/ALeqM5jLC_KNXJtRGZeKjUaaSJiaEcWkJA
2. Paul Handley, "Red Teddy Bears on Valentine's Black Market in Saudi," AFP, February 13, 2010, http://www.google.com/hostednews/afp/article/ALeqM5hQgas-214FBy0bjpdxhtP8dmhQOQ

Books

Bronson, Rachel. *Thicker Than Oil: America's Uneasy Partnership with Saudi Arabia*. New York: Oxford University Press, 2008.

Keating, Susan. *Saudi Arabia (Major Muslim Nations)*. Broomall, PA: Mason Crest Publishers, 2009.

Schaffer, David. *Saudi Arabia in the News: Past, Present, and Future (Middle East Nations in the News)*. Murray Hill, NJ: Myreportlinks.com, 2006.

Temple, Bob. *Welcome to Saudi Arabia (Welcome to the World)*. Mankato, MN: Child's World, 2008.

Yackley-franken, Nicky. *Teens in Saudi Arabia*. Bloomington, MN: Compass Point Books, 2007.

Works Consulted

Abramson, Larry. "Saudi School Aims to Save the Planet." NPR, May 4, 2010. http://www.npr.org/templates/story/story.php?storyId=126484992

Al-Yassini, Ayman. *Religion and State in the Kingdom of Saudi Arabia*. Boulder, CO: Westview Press, 1985.

Arabian Mythology http://www.jrank.org/cultures/pages/4945/Arabian-mythology.html#ixzz109IKYvvz

Beyer, Lisa. "Osama's End Game." *Time*, October 15, 2001. http://www.time.com/time/magazine/article/0,9171,1101011015-178412,00.html

Bowden, Rob. *Asia*. New York: Gareth Stevens, 2005.

"A Brief History of Arabia and Modern Saudi Arabia" http://www.mideastweb.org/arabiahistory.htm

The Carolina Center for the Study of the Middle East and Muslim Civilizations http://www.unc.edu/mideast/index.shtml

Center for Defense Information. "Spotlight: Al Qaeda." *CDI Terrorism Project*, December 30, 2002. http://www.cdi.org/terrorism/alqaeda.cfm

CIA, *The World Factbook*, "Saudi Arabia" https://www.cia.gov/library/publications/the-world-factbook/geos/sa.html

Dekmejian, R. Hrair. "The Rise of Political Islamism in Saudi Arabia." *Middle East Journal*, volume 48 (Autumn 1994), pp. 627–643.

Dunjie Houston, Drusilla. *Wonderful Ethiopians of the Ancient Cushite Empire*. Forgotten Books, 1926. http://www.sacred-texts.com/afr/we/index.htm

Earth.org. "Open Travelguide." http://www.earth.org/travel-guide/Saudi-Arabia/flora-fauna

Handley, Paul. "Red Teddy Bears on Valentine's Black Market in Saudi," AFP, February 13, 2010, http://www.google.com/hostednews/afp/article/ALeqM5hQgas-214FBy0bjpdxhtP8dmhQOQ

Hitti, Philip K. *History of the Arabs: From the Earliest Times to the Present*. New York: Macmillan, 1951.

Long, David. *The Kingdom of Saudi Arabia*. Gainesville: University Press of Florida, 1997.

Nawwab, Nimah. "About Nimah I. Nawwab." http://www.nimahnawwab.com/about_nimah.html

"No Love for Valentines in Saudi Arabia," AFP, February 13, 2008. http://afp.google.com/article/ALeqM5jLC_KNXJtRGZeKjUaaSJiaEcWkJA

Ochsenwald, William."Saudi Arabia." *In The Politics of Islamic Revivalism: Diversity and Unity*, edited by Shireen T. Hunter. Bloomington: Indiana University Press, 1988.

PBS. "Pilgrimage to Karbala—Sunni and Shia: The Worlds of Islam." *Wide Angle*, March 26, 2007. http://www.pbs.org/wnet/wideangle/episodes/pilgrimage-to-karbala/sunni-and-shia-the-worlds-of-islam/1737/

Salibi, Kemal. *A History of Arabia*. Delmar, NY: Caravan Books, 1980.

Serafin, Tatiana. "The World's Richest Royals." *Forbes*, June 17, 2009. http://www.forbes.com/2009/06/17/monarchs-wealth-scandal-business-billionaires-richest-royals.html

U.S. Department of Commerce, International Trade Administration. "Saudi Arabia." *Market of the Month*. http://www.trade.gov/press/publications/newsletters/ita_0307/saudi_arabia_0307.asp

U.S. Department of State, Saudi Arabia http://www.state.gov/r/pa/ei/bgn/3584.htm

The White House. "April 1 – April 29, 2010: Hub Activities Report." http://www.whitehouse.gov/sites/default/files/microsites/ostp/04292010-newsletter.pdf

On the Internet

BBC News, Country Profile: Saudi Arabia
http://news.bbc.co.uk/2/hi/south_asia/country_profiles/791936.stm

HAJJ—Pilgrimage to the House of Allah in Mecca
http://www.islam.com/hajj/hajj.htm

Lonely Planet
http://www.lonelyplanet.com/saudi-arabia

The Royal Embassy of Saudi Arabia
http://www.saudiembassy.net/

United States Department of State, Background Note: Saudi Arabia
http://www.state.gov/r/pa/ei/bgn/3584.htm

Washington Post, Country Guide: Saudi Arabia
http://www.washingtonpost.com/wp-srv/world/countries/saudiarabia.html?nav=el

PHOTO CREDITS: Cover, pp. 1, 3, 12, 14, 18, 20, 23, 26–28, 30, 31, 35, 36, 40–42, 45, 47, 50, 51, 54—cc-by-sa-2.0; p. 2—Charles Roffey; p. 6—Philip Turner; p. 24—Amaud Desbordes; p. 31—Mo Elnadi; pp. 32, 37—Waleed Alzuhair; p. 38—David Hume Kennerly/Getty Images; p. 48—Tom Olliver; p. 52—Dr. Zaro; p. 55—Omar A.; p. 61—Charles Roffey. Every effort has been made to locate all copyright holders of material used in this book. If any errors or omissions have occurred, corrections will be made in future editions of the book.

autonomous (aw-TAH-nuh-mus)—Independent.

blasphemy (BLAS-fuh-mee)—Disrespect for God or anything someone of a particular faith believes is sacred.

coalition (koh-uh-LIH-shun)—An alliance; a pact.

emir (ee-MEER)—Arabic for "commander." Males in Saudi families are referred to as emir, as are political leaders.

emirate (EH-muh-rit)—A territory or region ruled by an emir.

fatwa (FAH-twah)—A religious ruling.

Fertile Crescent (FUR-tul KREH-sent)—The agriculturally productive area of land arching from the Persian Gulf over the watersheds of the Tigris and Euphrates rivers in Iraq through the western coast of the Mediterranean Sea and into Egypt.

genie (JEE-nee)—The English version of the Arabic word *jinn*.

Hajj (HAJ)—The pilgrimage to Mecca.

hajji (hah-JEE)—Arabic for "pilgrim," someone who makes the Hajj.

imam (ee-MOM)—A male Muslim spiritual leader.

infidel (IN-fuh-del)—What fundamentalist Muslims call those who do not believe in Allah.

jihad (jih-HOD)—Holy war.

jinn (JIN)—In Muslim demonology, one of a class of spirits that inhabit the earth.

Koran (kur-AN)—The Muslim holy book, written by the prophet Muhammad as the word of Allah (God).

Levant (leh-VONT)—The land area between Mesopotamia and Egypt.

oasis (oh-AY-sis)—An isolated area of foliage in a desert. The plural is *oases* (oh-AY-seez).

paganism (PAY-guh-nizm)—Belief in many gods or none.

pantheon (PAN-thee-on)—The group of gods worshiped in a religion.

per capita (per KAA-pih-tuh)—Per person.

pilgrimage (PIL-gruh-midj)—A journey to a sacred place.

polygamy (pah-LIH-guh-mee)—Having multiple wives.

polytheism (pah-lee-THEE-izm)—Believing in multiple gods; the Greeks and Romans were polytheists.

scion (SY-on)—A young member of an important family.

secular (SEH-kyoo-lur)—Being separate from religion.

Semitic (seh-MIH-tik)—The language or people of Middle Eastern origin.

souq (SOOK)—An Arabic market.

subversion (sub-VER-jhun)—An attempt to undermine or overthrow authority.

ulema (oo-luh-MAH)—The body of mullahs, educated Muslims who are trained in Islamic law.

INDEX

Abdullah, King 18, 21, 22, 49
agriculture 40
Al-Hasa Oasis 26, 55
Al Musmak Castle 20, 52, 53
Al-Qaeda 23, 45, 46
Arabian Desert 8, 16, 25–26
Arabian Nights, The 19
Arabian Peninsula 9
Bedouins 10, 11, 15–16, 20, 27, 28, 29, 31
Bin Laden, Osama 23, 45–47
Burton, Sir Richard 51
camels 27, 28
Eid al-Adha 49, 50
Eve 10
Fertile Crescent 15
gold 40, 41
Great Nafud (desert) 25
Hajj 41, 49–50
Islamic calendar 10–11, 49
Jeddah 10, 54
King Fahd Causeway 54
Mada'in Saleh 54–55
Malhas, Dalma 35
Masjid al-Haram (Grand Mosque) 22, 49, 50
Mecca 7, 10, 16, 20, 22, 41, 43, 44, 49, 50, 51, 52, 53
Medina 10, 16, 20, 41, 44, 53
Middle East 6–7
Muhammad (Prophet) 10, 16, 21, 42, 43–44
Muhammad Ibn Saud 17, 19, 45
Nabataean Kingdom 54–55
National Day 51
National Museum 53
Nawwab, Nimah 47
oil 11, 17, 18, 20, 25, 38
Olympics 35
Ottoman Empire 11
Queen of Sheba 15
Rashid dynasty 19–20
red sand 24
Riyadh 17, 19, 20, 23, 29, 33, 39, 44, 45, 53, 54
Rub Al-Khali (Empty Quarter) 24, 25, 41
Saud, Aziz Al (Ibn Saud) 11, 13, 14, 16–17, 19–20, 21, 53
Saudi Arabia
- climate 9, 25–26
- culture 31, 32, 33–34, 35, 36–37
- economy 39–41
- education 30, 39
- emirates 10
- ethnic makeup 9, 29
- etiquette 36
- fast facts 13
- fauna 9, 25–26
- festivals 49–51
- food 33–34, 37, 40
- geography 9
- government 19, 21–23
- history 11, 14, 15–17, 18, 19–23
- holidays 49
- map 7, 8
- military 48
- music 33
- religion 7, 9, 10, 15, 16, 19, 22, 29, 34, 49–51, 52, 53–54
- topography 9–10, 25
- wildlife 9, 26–27
- women's rights 11, 30–31, 36, 37, 47

Semites 9, 15
Sultan, Prince Ibn Salman 46
tourism 41
Wahhab, Muhammad Ibn Abdul 17, 19, 20, 44–45

Kathleen Tracy has been a journalist for over twenty years. Her writing has been featured in magazines including *The Toronto Star*'s "Star Week," *A&E Biography* magazine, *KidScreen*, and *TV Times*. She is also the author of numerous books for Mitchell Lane Publishers, including *We Visit Cuba; The Fall of the Berlin Wall; Paul Cézanne; The Story of September 11, 2001; The Clinton View; Mariah Carey;* and *Kelly Clarkson*. Tracy lives in the Los Angeles area with her two dogs and African Grey parrot.